Burning My Father

For Leeland Farms
my father George E. Lee
my uncle John C. Lee
my grandfather Herbert M. Lee
my mother Irene Lee
and to all the women who have ever worked
the land with their men

Burning
My Father

Writing the Farm

John B. Lee

2014 Black Moss Press

Library and Archives Canada Cataloguing in Publication

Lee, John B., 1951-, author
    Burning my father / John B. Lee.

Poems.
Issued in print and electronic formats.
ISBN 978-0-88753-532-1 (pbk.).--ISBN 978-0-88753-535-2 (epub)

    I. Title.

PS8573.E348B87 2014   C811'.54   C2014-900565-2
                                           C2014-900566-0

Editorial and Design Team:
Alexandria Bouma, Emily Dobson, Lauren Farquhar, Taylor
Fratarcangeli, Lauren Hedges, Stefanie Lankin, Shannon McLaughlin,
Asil Moussa, Micaela Muldoon, Christine Scott, Rachel Stadder,
Stephanie Thompson.

Black Moss
EST. 1969 **Press**

Published by Black Moss Press at 2450 Byng Road,
Windsor Onatrio, Canada, N8W 3E8. Black Moss books
are distributed in Canada and the U.S. by Fitzhenry & Whiteside.
All orders should be directed there.

Black Moss Press acknowledges the support of the Canada Council
for the Arts and the Ontario Arts Council for its publishing program.

PRINTED IN CANADA

Photograph I

My father
younger than I am now
holds a ram lamb.

There is snow on the earth
in every direction.

My father is slim.
His face is smooth and dark
against the winter.

The horizon
stays in the distance
forever.

Table of Contents

Preface

I've hoed beans. Mowed hay. Painted barns. Slopped bogs. Thrashed wheat. Built houses. Broken cattle. Shovelled corn. Mucked pens. Dug graves. Stooked grain. Slaughtered hogs. Driven truck. Ploughed land. Burned stubble. Worked fields. I've painted barns. Thrashed wheat. Broken cattle. Dug graves. Worked fields. Cut boars. Shorn sheep. Bulled cows. Fixed fences. Watered livestock. Shown heifers. Polished halters. Blown stumps. Pitched straw. Culled runts. Trimmed horns. Wrung bulls. Castrated cattle. I've inoculated the sick and helped with the midnight calving hot to the shoulder in breech. I've done all that and more. And that was before I was ten years old.

I've worked hard and slept keen.

As a boy growing up on a farm, I knew what it was to feel dog tired and yet to work on into the gloaming of summer and then to sleep the sleep of angels. But I couldn't wait to leave. I looked longingly down the road and dreamed of adventure in the city. I thought I lived at the centre of nowhere. I've learned since then that there is no such a place. Nowhere is a state of mind. Everything I know about the world, I learned on the land. I was born a fifth-generation John on the land settled deep in southwestern Ontario by my great-great-grandfather and namesake, Irish John Lee. I betrayed my heritage and left the farm at eighteen to pursue a career as a teacher and a poet. Since I left the farm to become a writer, I've slept an ever-more bookish sleep of the idle thinker. It's been a long while since the deeply satisfying physical slumber of my straw-hand childhood. If, as someone once said, "It is the memory that keeps us sane," then I owe the sanity of my life to my childhood as a farmer's son.

On Being Told I Cannot Go In
the House that was My Home

I am
no longer welcome
on the farm where I was born
the long lane
now longer
the barns all fallen
into stone
the silo sick with toxic gas
the house
an unfamiliar kitchen
rimmed in Roger's oak
the sheep ghosts of a flock of cloud
woollening the blue refusal
of an unknown sky
the meadows patchy black
with vapour shadows
strange lanolin that oils the edge of light
the drifting fleece lines
of a shearing shade
the get of sire
voiceless in a heaven made anew by dawn
and her bleating moon
as white as chalk
I stand invisible as all the other
orphan children of a foundling wind
the unseen waterline below the land
the river stones of former spring
the summer harvest
a golden rumour of what's gone before
dark bounty of a ripened mind
the learned seed
that fattens what it bends
the storm creel
sweeps a broom of black-strawed wheat

to find the whereabouts
of sorrow and of woe
like Job, if I am oversaddened
by the gatefold of this lost hour
I also know
the pine stand is a broken comb
thinning over time to one last brittle tooth
to do the skull bowl's grooming under grass
the green amnesia
of every over-oldness
come to hollow-brow
mute mystery
where language has an absent tongue
the bell
its clapper gone
makes valleys ring
with every silent gong
oh—quiet heart
this place so pulsed by rain
that I am there
in wind-snapped empires of an empty step
I stride and climb
the way I've seen the shadow climb
in France I saw
how dancers candled on cathedral walls
might brush the inner spires
of a vaulted roof
and lift by force of dream
the brilliant shingles of far galaxies
what's wonderful in this
might also shake the cuff chaff at the door
or make grey mop dust
thistle down from open windows
like the seed kites of the soul
I am become this circumstance
in one circumference
half-way from four directions
heading home.

john b. lee

The Connection

We hang the hog from a lynching tree
for being what he is
hooks through hocks
and squirming.

Above him apples dream bad dreams
tucked in spring blossoms
with the terrible possibility of life.

The leaves shake
like a kitchen knife slow strutting the slats
of venetian blinds.

And the hog, wild-eyed
spills his blood by bucketsful
like a clumsy housepainter
while his voice
a gargled scream
slows to silence.

I am but a boy
and cannot manage the connection
between this event
and Easter Sunday dinner's
sweet pineapple ham.

There Are No Cows
on the Merry-Go-Round

The dreamy carousel
goes round and round…
a world, a calendar of seasons.

Laughter unraveling
its bright ribbons
in slow dizzy circles

and in a pool of music
in a pool of time
we drop like melancholy stones
too deep to hear
the ripples we make
in passing.

13

What Happened to Jack's Cow

She too understood
poverty
lean as apple-barrel staves
her ribs
and grateful to have been worth
a hill of beans.

What happened to Jack's cow was
she grew fat
as a Rubens lover
and married
the bull of the barn.

Gone moody as cocktail jazz
she counted the years out
in thankless calves
remembered Jack's small hands at the last
passing her up
and forgave him his magic beans
trickling beyond the slackened rope.

The Pig Dance Dreams

The man who dreamed
a pig
dancing on his chest
leaving pronged trotter marks
in the flesh
dancing to wrestle
his jowl
against a human cheek
pig saliva sudsing
at his ear
dampening his hair so it clung
to the straw tick
wondered
if God loved him enough
to send this lean razorback.
Every night
he came like a lover
to grapple and wear the man out
dancing on his corduroy ribs
poking him in the belly
snorting at his nostrils
hot pig breath
winding like a fetid river
into his lungs
until he was startled awake
clawing up
from sleep like a bird
in a chimney flue
to find no pig

but his hands smelled of swine
and his ears were tender screams
of swine
and his arms were bristling
angry with spiked hair of swine
and his mouth
had the taste of raw swine
his tongue lathered
with his own mad speech
his own fear pushed against his teeth
so he ached like the ribs of a cage
holding in some
live animal with the urge to rend
explode a prayer
along his jaw
"God! Take away this pig."
so he fell
into a pigless sleep
tame sleep lucid sleep with no room
for darkness
just a thin light always on
docile and cold as a fridge light
when you opencloseopencloseopenclose
the large white door.

The Cats Liked It Best
When Tom Was Milking

Tom, the hired man
would hang his head
against the cow
to milk
on the stool tipped in

but all the milk he milked
went black

with what dropped from his chaffed forearms
and from the brim of his old hat.

My mother'd
skim the grit like cream

and strain the rest so it was fit for cats
who liked it best
when Tom was milking
for then they got it all.

So much that they rolled their bloat
down to the barn
to sleep their gut away on feed sacks
like lazy uncles
snoring their buttons loose
in a drawing room

dreaming of Tom.

The Cold Event

I fell
through the mow-hole
into the hog's trough
that fit me
like a casket
measured out for children.

Into the slop
that porridged under the eating sow's nose
into the mush
that splashed her oinking face
like a plaster maker's bad day.

And there I lay
a grave digger's nightmare
all angle
of arm hooked over the rim
tough-rooted to the shoulder
and my heart
pumping in the centre
like a bobbed-for apple
and my brain blurry
as a voice talking under water
the old sow looking at me
as if the mow-hole
had given birth, stepping away
looking up as if she might expect
a twin.

The Zombie Cows
of My Highgate Home

I used to think
I could
affect the will of cows.
Be their Svengali.
Give them the hex.
Make my eyes into voodoo spirals.
My pupils into weird inner kaleidoscopes.
I could shuffle their thoughts
like marked cards.
Roll the loaded dice between their horns.
Oh I was a crazy lad.
Shaman of the barnyard. Manson of the herd.
I started with small telepathies.
I could manage
the tail flick
the flank shiver
like a breeze in a mug of coffee
the head swing
like someone trying to jostle
a bass fiddle
through a narrow door frame
the cowlick
where the hair swirled
to the tongue like the whirlpool
of a clock spring
busted through its case.
Day by day
I'd build them bone by bone
and hair by counted hair:
this army of zombie cows.
Took them through the motions
while cud froth
gathered on their well-chewed hay.

19

john b. lee

In a month
I had them milking themselves
leaving naught for the calf
but a dry teat hung like an empty glove finger
from the slack
for the gutters ran white
as the deeds of nuns.
I had them paw the earth
and bellow
mindless marines
I had them pacing fences like a dangerous borderline.
We were ready to lay low
any Christ
that came our way.
At night
they gored the moon
while I dreamed
the professions of war.

City Kids

They ask if cows have teeth
... and do they bite?

Almost proud of their ignorance
though they recognize the dung
as if it were a relative
coming to call ...

"What do they eat?"
offering french fries, sandwiches
a sip of coke
ice cream, some of the smart ones
whose grandparents are still on the land
struggle a clutch of hay
or if they're stupid, straw
poking it at the large nostrils
or proffer a hand cupped with sweet grain.
Most pet between the horns
and wince when their fingers
get knocked against a plank.

Girls stand back
and giggle behind their hands
when a cow arches to piss
so it splashes in the dust
and boys moo in the bull's eye
gather close to admire the horns
or measure themselves at the muscled shoulders
with military grace.

In all of this there seems the desire
to touch and tame
but they come away troubled
if and when they learn
that humans are just cattle in the metaphor
and cattle are not cattle at all.

The Circus Could Have
Used Such Cows

Sometimes cattle attempt
                    the impossible.

A cow
on her back in the ditch
treading sky
like a flipped beetle
death's sweet terror in her eyes
or
the bull
who died straddling a high fence
his spine arced
against the top board cutting across his lungs
like a scimitar
his notched belly, heavy on either side
bloated wineskins of unconsecrated blood
rocking the cradle of his bones
all night
under the sickle of a ruined moon.

Mind is
like the sky reflected in a river then:
the flow of water
the movement of clouds
the involuntary twitching of consciousness
that would unscramble
the smashed egg of the universe if it could.
But the clouds pass by
the river freezes
the sun goes down
and the eyes close.

The Bad Philosophy
of Good Cows

Like a sleigh ride it was
throned on the old wooden manure scraper
and circling
the cattleyard behind the chug
of the orange Case tractor.

Enough to jar your bite mark
like a shook-out string of pearls
watch the green engine housing
breathing gas fumes on the wind.

Round and round we went
in a careless carousel
bucking over ice and frozen straw humps
round and round
my small body beetling the angles
like the bent hands of a pocket watch
in a tiny argument
I battled dung heaps up and down
the roughhouse undulations all morning till noon.

Finally done I stand atop the rank accumulation
like the only king of castle cow chip
while the cattle ungather
like the frayed end of a rope
as cattle will when humans
are finished with their chores.

23

john b. lee

And as if to say
'Here's enough entropy to get you through
the toughest maize'
three heifers and a cow
lift their tails
and have a simultaneous silage
constitutional
on the clean cement
and their big dumb muzzles moo
their bad philosophy
at the empty winter heavens.

The Distant Loom

Grandmother draws the slubbing
from her distant loom.

She traces a vein of clay
that runs along her wrist
into the next county
surfacing near water.

Her slub is a brown clot.
Her wool is thick
with goldenrod and flax.
In her womb
granddaughter's musical voice
goes dead
if you cut the thread.

Jobs

My uncle and I
sit on the sheep
we've heaved upside down.

It wriggles and bleats
as if we mean to tickle
but my uncle
pops a sharp knife into its throat
so its cries gurgle
along the blade
where red eloquence spills a slackness
to the tip of its hooves
till it shivers to a final look.
Till blankness dusts its eyeballs
as my uncle slithers a slit along the belly
and rolls of gut steam to the earth

while my mother and sister
cut a dress pattern on the dining-room carpet
for the high school dance
on Friday night.

This Table

"It is better to be born
a sheep on this farm
than it is to be born a woman"
my gentle cousin says.

And instantly I remember the looks
given my mother and sister
when those sheep men
came to the dinner table
with their men's talk
their reverence for this year's crop of lambs.

And I know she is right
about those haughty stupid men
that journeyed five generations to this table
gave me my place in line
my privileged birthright
as master of the flock.

Certain Creatures There Are

The weaner
sticks his nose deep into the trough
and blows
playfully so the water bubbles
like a boy's milkshake

OOBLEOOBLEOOBLE
OOBLEOOBLEOOBLE

then he looks up at me
where I am grinning over the half door
something passing between us
something of the tease
something of childhood's undiminished mysteries.

The Kill

The butcher woman
from New York City
drove her long black Lincoln
into the field.

She opened her trunk
and selected a knife
blessed by the tzaddik

so casual
the sunlight-warm support hose
hugged a vein against her calf.
Her muscles
flopped against the bones of her arms
like the necks of dead chickens
while she stropped the knife.

She chose from the flock
one shearling so tame
she would have
slept at your feet
but dropped her trusting nonsense
and quivered
to the woolled tips of her ears
when the butcher woman grasped the tufted jowls
sunk the knife to the handle
in the throat
laid the carcass out
and spilled all the warm
into the grass
so the carbonadoed flesh steamed
even on the sun-bright day.

"I'll take these," she said
her beveled digits
sweeping the clover
from horizon to horizon
felling an entire flock in a single shadow.

Shearing

His back arched
like a pissing cow's
my uncle shears the upended sheep
then sets them aright
ridiculous as naked deloused humans.
Plaintive and banal
as children,
"M-m-m-m-other I'm-m-m cold," they cry.
Not pretty fools
but oafs away from the fleece heaps.
They shiver
under a yellow slice of April sunlight
as cool and distant
as a guttering star.

Pretend You Are Happy

There's a pig riot in the brick barn
and my father goes down
with a cane
down to where those shoats
are taking out their grievances
on one poor weaner
whose side is streaked with toothmarks
his skin already red as a bad essay.
They're brawling
punks who won't quit
driving their jaws in his gut
and circling
while he pants half dead
weaving and stunned where they jam
his ribs like a slammed gate.

My father
goes in there
prying their jaws back
like a hammer clawing tough spikes
but he wins, being human
and they, being pigs, lose.

What has this pig done?
It is the Lord's day, and everyone is pretending
they are happy—
everyone, that is, except pigs
who have made their loud objections
and children, bored with dull television
and the way the sun moves
so slow every Sunday afternoon
like a lazy bachelor looking for salt
in someone else's cupboard.

Mending Gate

for Robert Frost

Something there is that doesn't love a fence.
Pigs, for instance
will root cement slabs
from a mucky floor
to get at the world.
They'll worry the found interstices
the chinks
no bigger than a curlicue
will serve to prod their noses through.
They'll please
to heave at the slipshod gate
even as you watch
they'll snout-strike a gap
like convicts.
They'll dare their bulk against a wowing plank
the sow's gut plumping through the slats
till heave gives way
and the gate boards snap
into the garden
and then the pigs are free
flying along the squash rows
jowling down puddles of chomped tomato pulp
rasping beneath the greening trees
for windfalls

burning my father

till one sow
roseated by the way a soft lawn
can be rutted like slop
makes for the edge of the corn field
which is where we found her
asserting her three dimensions
on a cob
snatched down and off
and when she sees us she
crashes into the corn rows
running between the stalks
into eighteen acres of crop
and we chase her back and up
across and down
the labyrinth until she's lost
in a fenceless realm
where pigs fall off the edge of the world.

When we leave her alone
to mend the shattered gate
she finds her way
back standing, waiting to return
to the world she knows
waiting as if to say
"Good fences make good pigs."

The Carr Cows

Driving the cows back the lane
to the pasture

one calf got unintentionally culled
from the herd.

It was a Carr-cow calf.
The dam turned to where her wee one
bawled behind me

and without a beat
she charged
threading her horns in my armpits
and flipping me
out of my runners
over her back
like a hired man pitching a sheaf.

And I try to imagine
my own mother
doing that for me.

burning my father

A State of Gracelessness

Billy and I were
chasing pigeons
clapping their wings like evening gloves
under the barn hip
until I ran
treading over the mow hole
a wingless, waxless Icarus
plunging to splash in cow flap
a dozen feet below …
an airless conflagration in the wet straw.

The Poppy roan startled by this
fragment of human sky
suddenly wheezing in her dung
came to snuff me like a newborn calf
before she turned
to moo above the half door

and moo she did
a peasant mother's mournful oolularum
so loud
the cats stopped whipping their tails
over the white-washed mouse gnaws
and raced for cover.

My cousin
Billy saw me there
in my strangle of straw
and went whimpering to tell my parents
I was dead.

john b. lee

By the time they came
to find me
I was standing
my small body shivering
and shit-brown
like a reflection in the muddy Thames.

My mother merely
made me go and shower
but the roan poppy
worried the whole night long
bellowing

under a sustained and wild applause
of pigeons.

Mother's Day

Every morning
I was wakened not by cock
nor crow
but by the traffic
of cows

walking legless in the tall water grass
under my bedroom window

calling up to me
like Cockney apple girls

calming the light
at the glass
like cooling the melt of yellow wax

there are certain transparencies
I cannot see through
sleep is one
memory another

and I remember everything
and I sleep often

though now I wake to clocks
that have a hundred hands
too many numbers
too much foreground
too much sunlight

john b. lee

The Loading

A single sheep
not yet loaded, and
what do the others do?

Thunder down the ramp
to join the loner
in the yard.

Either
the sheep on the truck
are friendly
or the sheep on the ground
has power.

Runts

My father
sends me into the sty
to kill runts.

I watch
the plump ones
nuzzling the sow for milk
feeding like carnivores
rending a recent kill
ramming her belly
with their hungry mouths.

Then I look
to the weak ones
congested, wobbly, angular with emaciation.
Their dry snouts
rooting impotently in the straw
their hunger real and undirected.

Never
robust myself as a child
never
did I suspect
that someone might have watched me
in the cradle
and wondered
if he should grab me by the leg
and beat me
against the doorframe
thusly.

Make room
for the strong.
Make room
for the heinous urge
of immortality.

There Are Such Rivers

Sheep trails look like rivers
from the sky
but sheep don't flow.
Nose to tail
picking their way foot over foot
they plod
dreaming a long drop
till, arriving, finally
they fan out
like a white stain
on green clover.

Sheep
eat scotch thistle
sow thistle
Canadian thistle.

If hunger
is great
sheep eat
barbed wire.

Sheep
never imagine
wolves.
They sleep quietly
counting
on tomorrow.

Sheep
empty themselves
into the dusk
their open eyes involving
headlights.

Pig Dentistry

i

My father picked up each piglet
tucked under his arm
like a small watermelon
calmed the squirming
with the certain strategy of his strength.
The razor-sharp trotters
striking out from forelegs
scored his ample belly
with a red welt
like a surgical scar
healed over a missing organ.
My father grabbed these legs
running in air
stilled the surge when futility finally occurred
to the pink little thing
with radiant ears
the light shone through
ears like a bride's nightgown
in the bright bulb
that swayed like a hanged man on its cord
in the sty.

Then he took the wire cutters
from his hip pocket
and opened the pig's mouth
blunting the scream with the size of his hands
and the imperative of his pliers
went snip snip snip
sizing the black teeth
that would needle-price the sow's teats
like a bad tattoo if they weren't taken
and I see them flying from the mouth
snip snip

like little wire ends they flew, making Gabby Hays
piglets, gummy at the back of their snouts
where they could have ripped your fingertip off
like the corner of a potato chip bag.

Then he sets them down
where after a moment's static revving
of their small hearts
they spin away
spitting out the remnants
of my father's dentistry.

ii

What would they have done
in the pre-domestic wilderness?

Made a horrifying shredded rag of her udder?
Pinkened her milk
like berries in breakfast cereal.

We live in such a humane society.
What would those of you who might call him cruel
have him do?
Lend his mind
to the prettifying makers of pork commercials.
Produce quirky little Disney movies
with all that damned big-eyed goodness
as if a boar could not tusk you open
so you spilled like wet groceries
from your own belly skin.

What would you have him do
for the sake of your delusions?
Starve you?

Stickless

The old boar could smell fear
in a human
like fire in a rag
so his legs poured to a gallop
his trotters clicking their engines
intent on the surgery of the tusks
to try a man's flesh
to test his cosmic tailor
by the zipperload

but Tom always
carried a sawed-off
hockey stick
for that boar, he'd come frothing
across the grass
at any man stupid enough to go
stickless

but he learned
to give Tom room.
The small thunder of a Koho cracking
across his snout
rattled his tusks
and buzzed his teeth to the very roots
once too often.

So he learned
a man with a stick
is a man to be reckoned with.
A man with a stick
is a man
not to be contradicted.

john b. lee

Hit and Run Companions

i

The first time I died
was in circles, a pebble
dropped in a pond.

Driving my motorbike up the lane
hit by a sheep

who laughed
like a bad comic
like a kid
breaking windows
like Miss Havisham
at Phillip Pirrip
like a mad nip
in a WWII flick.
Laughed till the wool stained
black with tears.
Laughed like crushed velvet
against a starched crinoline
while I tumbled and wore my flesh raw
against the gravel.

I was eighteen
and hadn't learned to savour pain
so I stood up
picked the cut stones from my flesh
like pecans from ice cream
hurled them red
against blue heaven
and sheared the silence with my curses.
Struck down by a sheep—
is this any way to die?

ii

Driving up the lane
to watch hockey
on his father-in-law's TV
he hit a sheep.

Fender scored skull
so death rushed
from forelock to fetlock

in a mad dash
along
nerve rivers
freezing as it went.

At the wheel
of the machine
trained by his own feet
he was as sorry
to have killed
as the sheep
was to have died.
Instantly
transforming itself
into a piece of paper
which could perform miracles
in a court of law.
Which could turn itself into vengeance.
Into money.

45

Sheep
if this is your idea
of a joke
then God bless
the humourless silence
of turned-under things.
God bless
the laughterless gravity
of serious shepherds
who check the clearing for vultures
and grieve
the gutless fleece upon the ground.

When I was in High School

Some said PIGS
were the easy bee-hive girls
with bouffant hair and mandrill face
breasts like candy cones in tight cashmere
that caught each lifted nipple like a licked gum drop
and skirts
that clamped the thighs in bondage.
And some said PIGS
were the uncouth futzing belching
ass-pinching jocks
with toothless grins like moonshine bootleggers
and all the vocabulary for vulgar sex
but none of the style.
And some said PIGS
were cops
gone bad and beating skulls
like home-run dreams
and flailing the grain of flower-children
till they broke on the threshing floor.
And some said PIGS
were presidents
and some said soldiers
and some said the rich
grunting in their coin under
splintered lamplight
fondling money-voiced Daisy Buchanan debutantes
tittering and vapid
while children starved
amidst the hot struggles of the poor.
And some said PIGS
were the establishment
whole governments, entire nations of swine
one fabulously crooked sty from sea to shining sea.
But few said PIGS are US, few could admit to
the oink they'd made
though the oinking they'd made was loud

john b. lee

a damned signature
for either we're all PIGS under the skin
looking out or looking in
or we're one glorious masquerade
and the world wears us
to d/r/eceive the gods.

The Police

When he came rapping
I was napping.

Kidnapping.

I could see him
from my upstairs bedroom window
standing at the front door
his riot helmet
straying on a randy knot of wool.

He was short and dumpy
freshly scrubbed and deticked
his blown-dry fleece
puffing from his uniform
he looked like a plump cloud
stuffed in blues.

But I know those sheep police
are pretty hard nosed

so I stumbled down stairs
and opened the door.

"You're under arrest!"
he said
his brain rustling behind that bony forehead.

"What's the charge?"

"Satire," he said
snapping his hay-stained molars
importantly
on the trumped-up charge.
"It's even worse than irony
in this here state."

I was in no state to argue.

I pled guilty.

I spent six years
in the pen.
The sheep pen.

Now that I'm out
I'm sure I'm under surveillance.

Undercover sheep
bleat into their pasterns
every time I cough.

So I watch myself.
I keep clean.

I wear wool sweaters.

If they think I'm one of them
I'm safe.

The Slaughterhouse Field

Sweet smell
of
blood wind
in the slaughterhouse field.

Drums of gore
in the back of the little white building.
Offal looped like sunning snakes
the colour of undertongues.

Puddles lit with oily rainbows
in the dung-middle.

Animal screams climb air
like the shriek of fire in a wet log.

Here
where hearts crowd a bucket
like buttons in a button jar.

john b. lee

There Are No Blue Cows

Belgian blue

blue roan
blue cow

moaning like low-down jazz

or a woman coming
in a tenement stairwell.

If I could get
my arms around the world

I'd make a niche for you
to ride the pulse
of my inner wrist
like a nurse's fingertips
and all the metaphors for counting
would be measured out
in blue.

The Nutting

I look at the toothmark dimple
in my father's Kodiak boot
the tiny divot
in the blond leather
where the sow made her impression
her head cocked
her mouth snapping and frothing below his sock top
while he nutted her sons
and tossed their testicles in the straw
like a shaken plum tree.

My job is to hold the wriggling piglets still
while he slashes the scrotum
so the purple cojones pop out
to be sliced free
but I can't take my mind off that sow
rushing in and out
like a grunting sumo wrestler
who dares once to bite my father's heel
then I jump the boards
crazed with fear.

My father merely clubs her snout with his elbow
and hurls another severed gland over his shoulder
so she turns to gobble the delicacy
distracted from her son's distress
by the prospects of deliciousness.

I crawl ashamedly over the partition
like foam boiling from beneath a pot lid
to spill my body beside my father
one eye on the sow, one eye on the squirming piglet
gripped before the slash
and my third eye
turned inward
like a testicle lost in the straw.

john b. lee

Pig Roast

The evening bends close
like a secret-telling girl
and the shadows
fit their form

while a suckling turns slow on the spit
and people move in the smell
on the perfumed hill
by the house above the embered pit.

The flesh is sleek on the hog
in the heat
and the door claps once and the door claps twice
on the porch next to the pool
near the field at the road
where breeze is calm as a priest
who blows a candle out.

One voice rises above the low talk
talk low as the softly mothering cluck
of hens in the dark
the voice of a ghost broken
on the wheel of life
who hung her hurt self
like a coat in the closet
alone she mourns unheard in the beer
unheard in the drunken sway of a branch
unheard in the cutlery click and the clink of glass
unheard in the tired splash
of a single swimmer's arm
unheard in the gay sizzle
of fat in the fire
where the hog holds to the spike in his roasted mouth
like a single word sharpened
in the heart of his head.
Guinea Pigs in the Hayloft:

Guinea Pigs in the Hayloft:
A Tale of Lost Virginity

How they studied
in the musty school of the hayloft
by the guinea pig pens
in the priestly feel

lifting aside
the heavy gate of their youth
beneath
the intermittent choir of pigeons
mothering in the scattered dark

blemished with light
that bled
in shafts through nail wounds in the sheet
and marked the floor
as with a coin worn thin.

It was not love
that made them walk sockless
on the fish-spined floor's cool sift

the gentle tug of petals holding on
their dry lips
touched and parted
while each heart plunged like an unhooked rose
down, down in
the little pink-bricked well
of their being.

They embraced and fell in the naked brush of green
their bodies entangled
like kite string
caught in the high black branches of their need.

55

john b. lee

It was not for love
but the cleft that made her female
pressed in white silk
like a kiss in a Kleenex
and for the stalk of his manhood that grew dangerous
and sticky as jam on a shirt cuff.

And he found her blunt thorn
and crafting a pearl in her wound
felt the faint flares of light
in the softly draining amazement of her eyes
like the slowly spreading stain of crushed berries.

No, they could not live
within the smoking contours of that day
when the snowless grass was furred with dusk
like a squirrel pelt
where they moved in their separate bodies for the light
that
wept
from a far warm kitchen.

The Old Cow Blues

The old cow moos
in the night.

She thinks of Billie Holiday.

She has the kind of blues
you get from heroin.

In her meadow
each cow flap
is a market busy with grubs
that shunt their exoskeletons like boxcars
under a whiskey-coloured moon

while the thick dawdle of each note
sustains against the starry silence
like a slow hot rush of subway air
and is gone.

Shouting Who We Are

After chores
the inconsequential continent
of my father's discarded clothes
dusts the cold shed floor.

Hog-smell perfumed
with the talc of chop
puffed into the sleeves from leaning on the hopper
caught in the fine sift of their hunger
pigs nudge his boots from the trough rungs
and skid through a scarf of straw
circling like someone setting a pocket watch twenty-three
hours wrong
then collapsing where he walks
rubbed from knee to cuff
by their hock-tinged paradigms of dung
and the bristled fabric of their hams
they race
breathe wet-snouted into the stuff he's left behind
their tongues powdered like and unlicked chalk gutter.

One miffed porker crabs the door
so it kicks on its hinges
while five cylindered noses
make a pink daisy chain
in the chink of light
between the door-bottom and the cement stoop.

Not a lawyer
who hangs his weskit on a chair
loosens his tie, and stagily rolls up his sleeves
to address a jury.
Not a doctor
who wears his stethoscope
like a sacred necklace
touching the cold amulet to your heart.

Not a poet
bangled and rapt
buying the death of each brief moment
with the coins of his eyes
and the coin of his word.
Not a mortician
with the sad slow droop of his hands
draining from each stiff white cuff
like something frozen while it flowed.

But a farmer
up from the barn
unafraid of his nakedness
the shower raining in the little gutters of his flesh
swirls in the drain mouth
milky with what it has meant
to live this day
as we all live with it
shouting who we are.

On the Way Home
from the Meat Factory
I Decided to Be a Poet

On the way home from the meat factory
I decided to be a poet!
Because sausages hung
like the long braids of Slavic girls.
Because the old herd bull
took the worm of the bullet
in his skull
and fell like a dynasty.
Because the hogs
caught death on electric floors
and jittering were dragged still warm
in their fit's-midst
to be halved like apricots
with their blue guts spilling
a circus clown's nightmare on the floor.
Because their heads came severed
like hill fighters
for the deli.
Because the purée came oozing into plastic tubes
cinched and cut
cinched and cut in log-lengths of cold meat.
Because the cattle fell
like drunks in metal stocks
then were carbonadoed and hung to cure
in the time it would take
to light a cigarette in the wind.
Because blood spilled in the gutters
under the peeled beasts
and ran bubbling still hot
for the reservoir.
Because the chainsaws whined in bone
like a mosquito night
and the bandsaw cut clean portions
marbled with fat.

Because I hunger.
Because the hand that cuts the meat
feeds the city.
Because I hunger
and am human
on the way home from the meat factory
I decided to be a poet.

Darkness Visible

Sometimes cattle lie
like mother's uprooted onions
left all day in the sun.

And they seem to worry not
about meaning
when they lift their heads
to lick their flanks
or switch their tails about
to cast off flies.

Yet God made men
not to imitate the dark
but to be the briefest light
flickering
making a greater darkness
visible beyond.

john b. lee

Jimi Hendrix
in the Company of Cows

i

Mooooooo
                    oooOOoooOoo
oOoOo
        o
        o
OOOOOOOOOOOOOOOOOOOOOO
                        O
                            oOo
OoOoOoOo
mmmmmmmmmmmmmmmmmmmmmmMMMMMMMM
MMMMMMMo
ooooooooo
oooooooooooooooooooooooooooOOOOOOO
OOOOOOOOOOOOOOOOOOO
mm ooo   mm ooo mm oo
                        mmmmmmmmmmmmmmmmmm
mmmmmoooooooooooo
n!

ii

Listening to *Band of Gypsys*
in my bedroom
while the cows maul their calves
like all-day suckers
sticky bulls-eyed clockwork springs of red-roan hair
that swirl like soft ice cream.
Machine Gun chords
strafing the fence line, music drifting
out the windows, out over the cattle
maple tree shakes
and fastens the
sky
to the edge of the barn, heifer works an itch, stamps
off flies, Jimi rides his red guitar
over all sniping pebbles into whirls of air
New Year's Eve, 1969, photographs on fire
the same summer I sit on the edge of my bed
with flames in my hair
cows outside — lifting their jaws from the grass
pause to consider
as if they smelled smoke.

65

john b. lee

First year university
I *Electric Lady-Land*ed my roommate too much
so one day he came in
like an operant-conditioning chicken
playing a wall of lights
bantam rooster strutting
lifting the needle from the groove
so it made that telltale
"zzzzreeeeeeekkkk!" I cannot spell
and "1983... A Merman I Should Turn to Be" was never the same
after that, skipping in the drumbeat
an erratic cardiogram, Mitch Mitchell losing sight of his hands, stumbling into the drum kit
like a strip-joint punch line ...
some would say it was the stale-sweet marijuana smell
in my jacket
and some would blame the recreational alphabet
I consumed like language in the dreamscapes of Chagall
but for one year I dove into the music
into the black concentric pools of vinyl
into the stereophonic roulette
the sound swirling in the headphones
like a marble in a milk pail
from the September he died
till the terrible ice-cube bath hot June in Paris
till my father came to me
telling me I was no good, in the bull yard summer
the smell of manure high in the air
miles from the edge of the world.

There Is No Fourth Wall

Dogs fly by the window
and cows play tuba
in the courtyard.

There is no fourth wall
in a poet's skull.

Crows consider their predicament
hung as they are like heavy fruit
in the high maple branches.
Birds startle from a bush
like a ruffled deck of cards.

There is no fourth wall
in a poet's skull.

Some accident of birth has left him open
like the pulsing soft spot
of an infant's cranium.

Let the mad grass
dream its green hosannahs
outside of where the earth's grown bald
from human commerce
in the park.

Let weeds draw up their contract
in the flower garden
like powerful men with too much money.

Let unattended cars explore the street below his window
like too many beetles shunting in a sugar bowl.

He is drawn to tipple the world
and language
stitches the water
like the circling ripples made
when droplets fall from the lifted mouths
of drinking cattle.

Oh Ye Cows Bear Witness

When I was stalled outside of Orangeville
on a dirt road I didn't know
on a Sunday, far from home
and mad
as a tiny nation of bees

I stormed the car
threatening the tires
kickboxing the door
yanking at life support systems
thinking oil, hmmm
fumbling a flight of wingnuts
into the deep dark abyss of the engine

I scrambled for weapons
cursing in solitude, or so I thought
until I turned
and saw
the audience of cows
which had gathered very quietly
behind me
drawn by the theatre of my rage.

They stood
ruminating on their cud
almost impressed
with the pyrotechnics …
a brief fury at the pasture's edge
signifying nothing.

69

john b. lee

Her Dairy Princess Sensibilities

Her flesh as white and fresh
as milk newly squirted
into a jar
she listens blushing to the violence
in my verse
and worse, she thinks me crabby
with slaughter
so much so, the fabulous blood dribbles down my chin
or weeps from her struck ear.

She wonders why I'd ring her skull
like a cow-kicked pail
with such ugly visions.
Why I'd want to leave the lid off a pasteurized world
for she's come to expect
that even the flies
will wipe their feet on the welcome mat
before they walk across her butter.

Eating the Young

With her nose, sow humps her nest
clean, dry, warm
as the inside of a careful woman's purse
left beside her
where she sits, one hand across the leather.

Then she flops
with a tired woomph of air
gently grunting as if asleep
to bring forth one, two, three –
then a final nose blinks, pausing
through the pink petals of her sex
like the tongue of a sassy girl …
four piglets to suckle
the fat-American democracy of her teats.
Four, only four
born to articulate her milky abundance
each a little lord or lady at a banquet table
heavy laden.

My father, ever the egalitarian pragmatist
takes two runts
from a half-ruined washboard-lean matron
with a litter of fifteen
and offers them the bounty
of this plump mother
rich with sap
each nipple pearled with a tear of its own excess
her young already glutted
flung like wineskins in the heat lamp.

These feckless nurslings teeter
towards her and she lifts her head
sniffing their strangeness
like fire in the straw
then she rises in rage and murders them there
her jaw snapping shut on the little chucks
like a half-set trap too strong for little hands.
This done she settles to sleep
by their corpses bent and tipped
torn-eared and dead as the moon.

Her own young awakened by the curious noise
lift their full bellies and walk
to explore the puzzling lukewarm stillness
in heat-fading flesh
enough
they turn and nuzzle sow's udder and
half-bored by the taste
bang her gut with their snouts.

Sestina on a Cattle Truck

for Blake Farren and William Blake

Riding in the back of a transport truck
With all the sheep and jostling tethered cattle
Where cigar-mouthing half-mad Blake
Leaning into the high-piled hay and rattling pails
Stood to mumble out a poem he'd been reciting
About a gopher in pasture just as green

As the breath of well-chewed hay is green.
And so we rode the highway in that truck
The metal sheeting shivering over the cattle
And over the words half heard from Blake
His hand resting on the bottom of a water pail
Yet though he'd drowned in noise, he stood reciting.

What he'd remembered as a child he was reciting
Now remembered as it were when he was green
In the back of Rankin's transport truck.
And Dan McGrew, though ghostly, bothered not the
cattle
Bathed in motion, they suffered not from Blake
Who thumped a steady rhythm on the upturned pail

Though the sheep were worried by his fist upon that pail.
They joggled at the gate for his reciting.
Ignored the hay though it were inviting green
And flocked into the corners of the truck.
But this was no concern to the tied-up cattle
Who sniffed the passing road ignoring Blake.

john b. lee

And so he went, this barded Blake
His words as hollow as if hallooed in a pail.
I know not now, nor knew then, why he kept reciting
The words he'd caught in air amongst the passing green
That took the silver we could see beyond the truck
And wind-snuffed highway moving underneath the cattle.

Yes, and groomed for show they were, those cattle
Groomed more finely than this sweating Blake
Who spat a final muggy stub into a water pail
As if it were a word not worth reciting
And mumbled out a line spit over-green
Inside the silence within the stopping truck.

Then open came the door on his reciting
From musty half-light onto the waiting green
We tumbled down the ramp and off that truck
Off that awful cattle truck.

Playing Dirty Pool
With Sacred Cows

This poem
is about things
which are very temporarily important
for people with memories as short
as a grocery list with only the word
MILK
written on it.

This poem is about cows
in a pool hall
their cheap halos
hung in the smoke
that weaves in and out
like angels sneaking away early.
Cows who lean
on the table, crack wise
and break the physics
of their species into something two-legged
chalking their horns
and learning to spit so it rings ...

while we humans fall on all fours
as if somebody suddenly dropped our
strings
and left us there to scrutinize
a pepper speck
in a wide flat veldt of sand
below the parched grass
where the cows pick up their cues
and knock the eight ball in the pocket
clacking like an old Underwood
staccato struck on a single key.

john b. lee

Cry

When they cut his horns
the blood wept
and followed the chines
down his face
leaving a changeless stain
below his eyes
so they called him Cry
though he was uncommon cross for a steer
not given to herding.

He moved alone
like a mad widow
marked forever
and remembered
without favour, without affection
but remembered.

The Pig Farmer's Wife

The pig farmer's wife
has three hundred pairs of elegant shoes.

They sit in her closet
till she selects one pair
then wobbles
out to the piggery on spiked heels
while the evening pumps
the sky with a billion stars
over the softish "sucketta sucketta"
of her stilletos in the muck
sour water brewing in the tiny wells
the counter eruptions that populate
each wound
with brimful uric liqueur
for the shiny beetle dine.

So there she is trotting the manurey glebe
with her spare shoes
cloistered like nuns in the little shack
one hundred and fifty miles from the nearest town
the vogue of the sty
but those trim-foot hogs
only stare and grunt, "Umpf?
What's that to me? I wish for nothing more
than cob and slop.
Why she splatters out
for this dumb ballet
as if she could improve the beast
with rhinestone
and make a better heaven of her feet
than those two odd stars
I count by looking up.
I wish she would but scuttle the dance
and litter the yard with winesaps."

Bay of Pigs – Photograph of
My Father Vacationing in Cuba

"The best pigs in Cuba"
he says, "would have been culls
in Canada."

I have an image of the way
we used to break the skulls of runts
like flawed pottery
so the lucky brothers would grow fat
on sow's milk
in the dishonest oligarchy of the sty.

Here in my living room
father shows me photographs
of fields
with crooked rows of etiolated lettuce
lying like faded pom poms
in the scar of shallow furrows
and in one picture
he is sitting in the shade
with a small green lizard on his pantleg
and I wonder
who will judge
the comfortable democracies
which measure out their money
like frugal shop girls buying cheap coffee.
Poverty has little consequence for the rich
charity is always tragic
that the lean dog is always the meanest
after a meal
and in the Bay of Pigs
for once, the swine recognized the pearls
and cast them back in the oyster-killing sea.

Translations from a Death

Beyond the slaughterhouse
the wind smelled of mortality
measured in heavy branches
that seesawed above the field
like drunken conductors
where creek water strategized its pebbled bed
ruttling in thin silver slivers
while each corn stalk shook its tambourine
like a narrow-hipped girl
learning the tune of summer.

All afternoon hogs were murdered
while the sun slept like a dragon on its shifting gold
and our slow wagon
swayed lazily above each tire rut
moving half empty
beneath crow shadows that flicked
like drugged eyelids on the air.

My heart
rides the troubled ship of my bones
in search of harbourage
not quite so human.
Not quite so frail.
Not quite so full of blame.

A Glass of Milk

A glass of milk
is the kind of clock I fear
timing your dinner
timing your life.

Almost see your teeth grow strong
and white ...
your bones lengthen in the sleeve
your height marks
inch up the doorframe
like water lines
in a heavy rain

and the great bittersweet sadness
settles
like a drifting net of tree shadow.

Though you smile
through a milk moustache
licking your face like a kitten.
My boys
my proud young men
if I last till your hair thins
please leave me these moments
till then.

A Game of Pig

I had hoped that nothing would change
and that we could spend every stolen hour
as we wished
a family, gathered around this small table.

My mother-in-law – the queen of clubs
my father-in-law – the seven of hearts
my wife – the queen of spades
and I the player
with the golden hand he never plays
fanned in my palm
the small multitude of card hearts fluttering with
possibility
like those of little girls at a strawberry social.

But we must surrender
what we have
accept the passing of the deal
watch
the cards fade
like washed out party dresses
until we too
take our place in someone else's afternoon of luck
at some strange and distant table
our own face
that of a king or mustachioed jack
covered
by the slow turning of a spade.

*Pig is a simplified version of bridge in which the
queen of clubs, seven of hearts, and the queen of
spades respectively are the three most powerful cards
if and when hearts are trump.*

Photograph: My Sons
and the Hog-Yard Pigs

The hog-yard pigs pose
graphed by fence wire
and framed by railway ties
in the hog yard beside the scalding house
where my uncle dug in the ancestral tel
and found an old embrocation bottle
once filled with horse liniment
the name welted on the clear glass
a message from the distant past
how the acres took their toll
on a working joint
but the ghost of geldings
have set their forehead stars
in the midst of multitudes
and shrugged the harness from their withers
like a puzzlement of apple branches.

So, these pigs too
cheese cut by the grid of fence
from snout, to poll, to ear tip, to jowl
to hock, to tail –
Yorkshire, Landrace, Tamworth
under the willow wisp
that hangs in the fall-blue heavens
like a heavy smoker's slender hand
and my two young boys
take the foreground with their smiles
dressed in coats
that haven't fit them for five years since.

I deny the falsification of time
with this 3 by 4 confirmation of the smallness
and this only known existence of proof
outside of failing memory
of these particular pigs
their souls stolen
like bolt ends of widow's cloth.

84

Isn't He Cute

Soul in that body –
smoke blown into a tea cup.
His angled face
sucked in by hunger
flesh hugging bone, jaw
a revolver stuffed in a handkerchief.
Pink-eye blind. Dead unseeing.
Pushing at my son's hands holding the bottle
a mouth insisting.
Jerks the rubber nipple
plucking, biting at the warmed yellow liquid.
Slamming its mouth against
the unveined udder of the glass mother
swallowing hard.
Its real mother dead a week
a wet nurse for crows
their sucking beaks.

And God, He's an old gentleman
who takes my son upon his knee, explaining
why he has nothing to fear.

Burning My Father

After the Beatles
our hairstyles grew Biblical
and the barbers went broke.

As for my father
one evening at supper
he said to me
"if you want to continue
putting your feet under my table
you'll go
and get a haircut."

Meanwhile at the meeting of the Ladies Guild
the church women
drove my mother to silence
over cake crumbs
and the money in tea
debating
the disrespectfulness
of long-haired youth.

My great aunt Isabel
wife to a dour
and sanctimonious Episcopalian priest
castigated me
for having respect
for neither God
nor country.

Men I'd known all my life
called me, "That thing! That
Hoochie Coochie girl."

I saw my bachelor uncle
drag a young man into the halter stall
at London Fair
where he ran the sheep shears
chattering up his red-scarred scalp
leaving him shorn from nape to crown
using the drunken excuse

"Long hair scares the cattle."

I've always listened well
for the ugly laughter
of nasty men.

My father's hair at the end
lashing his forehead
inching over the delicate bone of his nape
fringing his ears
spilling on the hospital pillowslip
feathering the linen like a new-plucked angel.

My sister
tossing a barn board
in with his body
gave the weight of his ashes
this additional smoke

trapped in the grave
beyond the last heartbeat of his being
his complicated love
and *my* forgiveness
given freely.

How important it became.